HEAT

Series 3 Number 4

Hossein Valamanesh
Breath 2012
bronze
143 × 140 × 5 cm
edition of six
courtesy of GAGPROJECTS and
the estate of Hossein Valamanesh

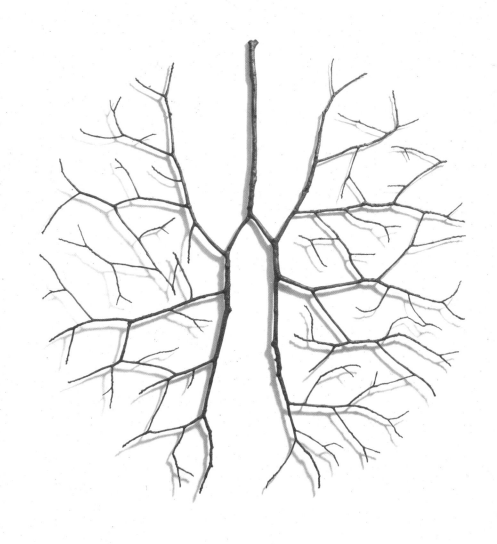

CLARE MURPHY
PIONEER SPECIES

Clare Murphy is a writer and editor currently completing a Master of Philosophy in Creative Writing Practice at Queensland University of Technology. Her recent and forthcoming work appears in *Westerly*, *Island* and *Unlikely*. She lives in Tulmur on the unceded lands of the Jagera, Yuggera and Ugarapul peoples.

DEAR RESIDENT,

This is how it begins – with a letter slipped under the door. With an architecturally inspired X for a logo, twisted into the shape of a house. With a brief black-and-white rectangle containing the words

all trees will be removed and the land will be levelled at No. 23.

I look up from the page to the neighbouring wall of trunks and fronds that spill over the chainwire fence, their bellies pressed against the chinks, rising and spreading, tall and riotous, so that our rented inner-city worker's cottage at No. 25 is hidden from passing cars and pedestrian eyes coming down the street.

It is true that the umbrella trees, with leaves that fan like whirring clocks, belong in Far North Queensland. That the cocos palms that fling their drupes across our roof have sailed across the South Pacific Ocean from Brazil, and that their unripened pleasures will lock the jaws of flying foxes in nights to come. That the fence-line forests of Chinese elms will continue to spawn rapid thickets of selfish shade. That these towering frenemies will keep drawing the celtis leaf beetle south and away from central coastal Queensland where it should be feeding on *Celtis paniculata*. I know that all these trees, out of their own communities, are weeds. And despite this knowing, I know I'll miss them too.

My partner, D, on the other hand, refuses to mourn the intruding canopy that has stunted his own gardening ambitions here in Meanjin's concrete-heavy heart.

'What about the gigantic hoop pine?' I say, going straight for his Achilles heel. (You need to play dirty if you're going to argue about weeds with an ecologist.)

He's talked before about how he'd replant right through

the neighbour's yard if he had his way. But the pine, which is endemic, gigantic, perennially festive, would be the only thing he'd keep.

Lying on the bed at the end of a long week in yet another long year, his fingers work at the tangled earbuds sprouting from his phone. 'The guy's a developer,' he says, pushing a bud firmly in one ear. 'He said *everything*.'

I offer words like *shade* and *privacy* but his ears are budded and, anyway, these words fall short of the darkness I'm trying to convey. It's not only about the shade. Or the chlorophyll glow of afternoon in our lounge room. Or the lorikeets that spill drunkenly, like scattered shards of rainbow into our yard as the sun slips its amber fingers around our sideboard ornaments. Or the glint of possums' moonlit eyes as they clamber along our roof and land with a whoosh in the leafy network of surrounding branches. Or that these will be replaced with stark walls and sharp light and battalions of mother-in-law's tongues in the months to come.

It's about the fact that, in the late summer of my life, I'm still a renter here. That I'm further away from belonging to the place than when I first moved to the suburb as a student over twenty years ago.

Dear resident,

That's me.

I'm not an architecturally inspired logo. And I'm not *Dear owner*.

And I will miss all the other life, like me, that increasingly doesn't belong here.

It is fitting that the meaning of the word 'resident' resides insecurely within itself, subject to the nature of movement that it seeks to represent.

It has come from the ancient Latin *residere*, to 'sit down, settle; remain behind, rest, linger; be left', in which the 're' once suggested that straying and returning was part of the lingering but has, in French and English usage since 1570, come to mean both 'to dwell permanently or [... to] have one's abode for a time'.

I have, indeed, had my abode for a time. Ten years, in fact. I have strayed to other suburbs and returned here where I had friends and work and habits of being. I have married once, young, divorced at nearly middle-aged and slipped down the rungs to home ownership in the years I spent afterwards as a single mother of three. And I have still not figured out what you do, as a resident, with your feelings, your needs, your memories, your morning coffee on the back patio crammed with guilty exotics. With your flock of chickens and ginger cat all buried in the soil where you reside. Or the life you still share the place with: the blue-tongue that sunbakes under the stoop. The striped marsh frogs that duel like plucked banjos in the plastic tubs you call a water garden while your head sinks into the pillow at night. Or the spangled drongo with its forked tail, flitting between the close-packed houses, taking you by surprise. What do you do with the unexpected reach of all this familiarity in a place you cannot afford to call your own? What does a resident do with all this when it is threatened?

A resident googles X to see what kind of developer he is, to assess the level of threat.

Gated elegance in the heart of Brisbane, his website boasts of a Bauhaus bunker with a green wall.

Reading this, something inside a resident feels as if it is taking flight.

Dear X, I write.

I go on to tell him all about us, his new neighbours. *The human face,* I call this. I mention exams. I mention work-from-home scenarios. The need to keep protruding eaves and air conditioners. I do not mention the spangled drongo. Or the beloved chicken bones beneath the overhanging Chinese elms. Or our own front garden full of local species that D spends his early evenings watering, backlit by western sun, swarmed by motes that bite.

Later, when I do try to tell him about this, it will be too late.

Landownership, writes Simon Winchester, has its origins in a 'point of unconformity'. From the moment a difference could be noted in the demarcation between here and there, then yours and mine, the settlers who first farmed Europe found a way to put a boundary to use. But it is how those that followed interpreted and enacted the rules around these unconformities that would shape the resulting cultural view of how humans should relate to their environments, to each other, and all they share it with. As the myth of terra nullius tells us, if landowners don't conform to the rules of acceptable use, colonising cultures find ways not to recognise ownership at all.

Before X came along, the cottage next door was owned by a long-bearded man who had lived in it for over thirty years and who was known to throw rakes at children whose bike tyres bruised his hot pink impatiens. He also called to have the footpath fixed when my aunt tripped on a minor tectonic rift that had, on impact, forged a mountain range along her cheek. Over the years, the man had become known for his habit of saving things, too many things, to the point of becoming one of the city's richest hoarders. It was he, with a twinkling zirconia nestled in his whiskers, who had nurtured the weeds that overtook three inner-city yards. It was he who reminded everyone that you can discard what you like but it will not just go away. Impervious to storm, flood, fire, rot, collapse, or the council, the things he saved persisted while change churned all around him. Perhaps this is why it seems so unfair that, in the end, it was scarcity (of land like his) that got him.

Landownership might have given our old neighbour the 'right of exclusion', but it did not protect him from neighbours who believed it was he who should be excluded.

After they finished removing his things, they had the man removed as well, making room for the gated elegance that the neighbours agreed belonged there.

Landownership, it might be said, ends just where it begins: at a point of unconformity.

Hi C, it's X from next door. I noticed that the arborists left a huge mess in your front yard. Can I clean it for you on Monday?? I hope this is okay.

Hi X – that's a lovely offer. D is happy to clean it up himself. He has a native garden out the front so he will do it, just to make sure nothing gets pulled out. But thanks for offering.

Hey C, I just wanted to let you know that the earth movers are starting today. They will most certainly stir up some dust. I see you have some white shirts on your clothesline!! [close call smiley face]

Yikes. Thanks, X. Will get those in before I head out. Thanks for letting us know.

Before our old neighbour went unwillingly into respite care, we'd already started to think about our near future as empty-nesters.

'We need to work out where we want to be in a couple of years when they bulldoze this place too,' I'd told D. 'We need a plan.'

We'd decided on the Sunshine Coast hinterland to help my cousin care for my aunt, and to be close to D's family who live there. We'd plant our own garden, plan our own shade, nurture a community – make our own decisions about whether or not we wanted curtains. It was somewhere we thought we could afford to buy. But then news of a novel virus spread, and many of those who could no longer travel decided they would spend their money on a tree change, on a place where they could work from home, taking advantage of the flood of cheap money, in the form of record low interest rates, that the government freed up for those who already had plenty. We watched the news, eyes boggling at the hinterland prices as they soared right through the canopies.

And then, because the mind has a way of fooling you back into whatever it thinks you need, I refashioned the plan, leaving out the parts that suggested I had limited options: Accept that you are already home, I told myself. Home ownership: the Australian dream. What is that, anyway? A bank. A taxation loophole. A superannuation fund. Accept that your home is here, where the currawongs who once visited from the mountains only in winter now fling pegs from your socks any time they like, where the brush turkeys run like startled dinosaurs through your neighbour's renovations. Accept that this place will not stop changing, but it is home.

The place in my mind, the home I'd been looking for, I told myself, fed only one story of myself – at the expense of all other stories. I suspected myself of writing what scholar Emily Potter would call my own 'sorry novel', looking to the 'redemptive possibilities of non-modern environments', hoping 'to redeem [my] fraught belonging and reclaim a rightful place, even if this is mediated through violent and discomforting pasts'.

Learn how to live here in this disturbed state, I told myself. Live with the edge dwellers – the ibis, the crows, the noisy miners – refuse to sweep away the past. Accept that perhaps, somehow, you are part of this place now in some dubious way. *Naturalised*, as the ecologist calls it, pervasive and persistent like the umbrella tree or the cocos palm or the Chinese elm but part of a system in a functioning state of its own, damaged as it might be.

This is how I resolved to outrun the terms of my residence. And for a while it actually worked.

It's a bright blue winter's day when the arborists' chainsaws fall silent and the earth mover putters out of the neighbour's yard. I look at what isn't left and I think about how hard an absence is to take in. How it's even harder to describe. You can start by describing what's no longer there. Or you can try to look harder to see what remains. Out the back, at the farthermost end of a beige expanse, I see the dead end our neighbour backs onto. I count four houses, two shrubs, two compact trees and an apartment building that were previously hidden by palettes of green.

'It's pretty bare, isn't it,' I say apologetically, on behalf of my species, to the pied butcherbird perched on the Hills hoist beside me.

It glares back at me purposefully before retrieving a mouthful of legs from the dirt. Then, in a black-and-white flash, it's gone again, reminding me that life is everywhere, whether one particular species sees it or not. From the leopard tree three houses down, the bird's melodic chortling sounds suspiciously like gloating.

'Acclimatisation in action,' I mutter to whomever might still be there.

When the next morning unfolds empty of brawling lorikeets or the crystalline bell of magpie, I convince D to come for a drive out of the city to the native plant nursery in one of the suburbs more committed to leafiness. We are looking for macarangas with their sprays of broad, heart-shaped parasols that will shoot up fast and fill the space where the umbrella trees outside our lounge room previously stood.

Macarangas are a tropical and subtropical pioneer species and, strictly speaking, don't appear in the government's documented list of rainforest plants that grew in pre-cleared Binkenba but our old neighbour grew them and we have already allowed two to spring up spontaneously in our yard. As a pioneer species, they are programmed to grow rapidly in areas of disturbance, until they are succeeded by the plants destined to form higher canopies after them, having grown under the pioneer's opportunistic protection. Birds also love the macaranga's continuous fruiting, and so, in these extenuating circumstances D is willing to turn a blind eye to the contextual ambiguity the list imbues them with.

We have crunched up and down the nursery aisles criss-crossing and double-checking for some time before we come to accept that the nursery is out of stock and settle instead for other fast growers: leptospermum which (with care) will shower us with multitudes of pollinator-loving blossoms in the

16

spring, and a wattle with determined, upward-pointing leaves whose sunshine fragrance I imagine wafting on the breeze and in through the living room window.

Afterwards at home, I skirt our parameters, digging up delicate cotyledons and holding them out to D in the hope that what I've found are the first embryonic signs of new macarangas. He confirms several, so I plant the strongest three between the seedlings we have bought and water them in along our side of the fence line, nestling rocks around them to ward off the brush turkeys who will indelicately taste test anything new. For a moment we content ourselves with the feeling that we have encouraged new life. We push away the thought that the day will soon come when the earth in this garden is moved and this life is ploughed into the ground.

When British cultural theorist Raymond Williams wrote about earth moving, he described it as a tool of the 'improvers', a class of people concerned with producing a 'disposition of nature' to suit their own mediated point of view, to serve either their 'practical' or their 'aesthetic' use values.

Williams, before his death in 1988, started a conversation that no one else has found a way to adequately finish. So, the conversation continues with some humans trying to figure out how to live in cities and square this with Williams' advice that we need to practise a sense of 'livelihood' which reconnects us to the entire web of life running through a place, to darn up the imaginary rift we've created between the concepts of city and country.

The ecological project D works on involves recording birds on rural landowners' properties, usually farmers', to help gain a clearer picture of an area's ecological state. A big science fiction fan, he's recently read Kim Stanley Robinson's *The Ministry for the Future* and become fascinated with applying its concepts to planet Earth. This means finding incentives for landowners to care for their 'property' in a way that creates steps to incremental, sustainable change and rekindles ecological connection. He trundles across farms in far western Queensland, listening for life, and when he comes home, he stands in the diminutive woodland he has cultivated on this inner-city land that another man owns and listens some more.

In our own small way, we have also moved earth. We have produced a garden that conforms to our own practical and aesthetic use values. It is an island of attempted restoration, floating disconnected from its surrounding context and the contexts it should join, defying any real opportunity to be of any combined natural and cultural benefit. We have created our own boundaries of what is acceptable. Our classification system, in its exclusion of Turrbal and Yuggera ways of knowing this place, and in the centring of a specific set of human values, is still a 'codification of the land'. We have, as writer John Kinsella points out, perpetuated the 'codes of occupation', participating in an ongoing form of colonisation. Of continued denial, forgetting, dispossession and erasure. Of continued insistence that one society – of one species – has the right to decide who or what belongs and who or what does not.

We've forged our way through shallow gravelly soil, looking to fill anything like a gap, forgetting to listen to what the gap might tell us.

I am still grappling with this when I meet X at our own forced unconformity with his machinery gnashing behind him.

'I'll put some turf down there for you,' X is shouting over the din.

He points at a bare patch the size of a grave that his earth mover has just torn along our front fence, past his boundary. I open my mouth then close it again. We have not agreed to this and an exclamation-marked text message has not arrived to warn me. The gravesite he points at is beside our garden gate where, until minutes ago, frisky white tufts of cat's whiskers glowed violet in the sun. Where blue-banded bees drifted upward to orbit constellations of native jasmine stars. Where flying foxes and honey-eaters plucked clutches of shiny black berries that spilt from twining spirals of kangaroo vine.

For three days now, our house has shuddered and groaned as his earth mover has bullied the ground into giving up crops of late Triassic rocks along the side of our house bordering his yard. Machines with flashing lights have buzzed and bleeped back and forth outside our windows, followed by men in high-vis vests hollering, examining, measuring, excising, removing any chainwire in their way. I feel jangled, on edge – threatened – as if a giant mechanical hand might reach down and remove me at any moment. And then I notice the seedlings we've planted to replace the lost shade and the privacy we'd prized: the pioneer species on our side of the boundary, bent and buried beneath builders' rubble, rock, and chainsawed chunks of umbrella tree.

'This,' I shout, stabbing a finger at the debris, 'is just not good enough.'

X's eyes follow my finger. 'I'm doing my best,' he shouts back, sweeping his arm towards the machinery. 'But this thing weighs twelve tonnes,' he adds, as if it's an uncooperative bullock he's wrangling.

'But this is the boundary,' I shout, stabbing again.

It sounds petulant and both of us know it. I imagine his text message back to the office.

X shrugs and I glare and we stand there with the earthmover growling and champing – the only living thing left in our midst. I look at the fashionable moustache he is growing before I look him in the eye. For a moment we stand there like this, sizing each other up with the noise and the dust billowing around us.

'The project of decoloniality is always unfinished and open-ended', writes the poet Peter Minter.

I take this to mean that the common language we seek will always harbour our histories. And that some weedy words are more noxious than others. Words that leave what Minter calls 'ideological traces' wherever they've been. Like *pioneer* with its assumption that none have come before, how it celebrates 'progress' and seeks congratulation on its struggles. We need only look to its origins in eleventh-century French to know that it was the word used to describe footsoldiers who cleared a way for invading armies. These are the traces that are hidden when we use such words to describe life – like 'pioneer species', who in fact grow in relation, not isolation – to ward off the fear of displacement my kind transported here.

It's true that those of us who haven't learnt how to belong find other ways to proliferate and rearrange things to hide this fact. In so doing, we lose the chance to learn what we can about a livelihood that might truly connect us to our environments, to take the ethical path that reminds us to engage.

I want to tell X that this is about *weeds*. About *residents*. About *ownership*. That we are standing on a faultline where the eruptive potential of our words cleaves meaning apart just as it cleaves meaning to it. But these are not words that should be shouted. Nor are they all mine to speak.

So, instead, I turn back to my rented worker's cottage and I shut the door on his noise and his dust and his ridiculous fashionable moustache. And in the sunlit lounge room I sit and I think about the story I'm telling as the ground convulses beneath me, wishing I could explain it to him as the poet, Kate Fagan does:

Here I dig
for a different language,
a new balm for the bruise
of lost opportunities

But the words I'm searching for do not come and I can do nothing but watch the gecko that is darting across the windows, leaving lines of tiny hieroglyphs in its wake.

Dear resident,

This is how it begins.

Sources

Peter Minter, 'Transcultural Ecopoetics and Decoloniality in Meenamatta Lena Narla Puellakanny: Meenamatta Water Country Discussion', *Transcultural Ecocriticism: Global, Romantic and Decolonial Perspectives*, Bloomsbury Academic, 2021.

Emily Potter, *Writing Belonging at the Millennium: Notes from the Field on Settler-Colonial Place*, Intellect, Bristol, 2019.

John Kinsella, 'A Rural Diary', *Overland*, no. 204, 2011.

Simon Winchester, *Land: How the Hunger for Ownership Shaped the Modern World*, William Collins, London, 2021.

Kate Fagan, 'Authentic Nature', *First Light*, Giramondo, 2012.

Raymond Williams, *The Country and the City*, Chatto & Windus, 1973.

Rod Giblett, 'Nature Is Ordinary Too', *Cultural Studies*, vol. 26, no. 6, 2012.

YANNI FLORENCE
TREES AND FENCES

Yanni Florence, born Melbourne 1965, is a photographer and book designer who has eight published monographs: *Self Conscious*, 2009; *Southland*, 2014; *Animal Life* 2014; *Street Porn*, 2014; *Immolation*, 2015; *HE IS IN THE CITY*, 2017; *Tram Windows*, 2019; and *Trees and Fences* (collection of ten zines) 2020. His work is included in the National Gallery of Victoria's collection and was exhibited at their Triennial in 2020–21.

These *Untitled* photographs are from the series *Trees and Fences* 2015–20 which was first exhibited at ReadingRoom in 2022. They show the interaction of trees and fences. Sometimes planned interactions and sometimes unplanned, and sometimes just by themselves.

Images pp. 25–33
Yanni Florence
Untitled 2015–
from the series *Trees and Fences*
archival inkjet prints
42 × 29 cm
courtesy of the artist and ReadingRoom

ELLA JEFFERY
FOUR POEMS

Ella Jeffery is a poet, editor and critic. Her debut collection of poems, *Dead Bolt*, won the Puncher & Wattmann Prize for a First Book of Poems and the Anne Elder Award, and was shortlisted for the Dame Mary Gilmore Award. Her poetry has appeared widely in journals and anthologies including *Best Australian Poems*, *Meanjin*, *Griffith Review*, *Island* and *Southerly*. She is the recipient of a Queensland Writers Fellowship, the Mick Dark Fellowship for Environmental Writing, and the Queensland Premier's Young Publishers and Writers Award. She lives in Brisbane.

Supertall

432 Park

If I wanted stillness, I'd build a bungalow.
Seeking more adventurous methods
of existence, I bought. Yes here. Unleashed
from the marriage contract, I craved
height and distance, the obvious forms
of power. Now I own a length
of this exposed nerve: in the news they report
on pewter faucets, nickel tubs lugged
from Italy, how far the building leans in breeze –
still agents rappel floor to floor, people
always moving in. My neighbours jitter
in their embossed jimjams when wind swings
us off true centre, but all I've wanted –
years spent homebound holding babies,
my life a circuit of stores and meals –
is risk. I like these skunky halls where trash
piles up and the concierge campaigns
for tips from baby millionaires. Nights I uncork
my body, recline in the tub's smooth shell
and claim what I'm owed: to be left
alone. Below, my neighbours polish
their lawsuits: one got spooked
in a stuck elevator – an hour's horror
over now, however much she showboats
in the *Times* – elsewhere a minor
flood, soaked Cezanne sketches, grenades

of trash exploding down the chute.
Who cares! I'm cut clean, a perfect fillet
on my own white plate, and so what
if most days my whole life sways a foot in wind?
I know how fast a house can move –
one day you're done with mothering
and told the deed is absent your name.
But here every tremor and leak
is mine: the weather's white lacquer, roar
of wind through lower floors,
all part of what I paid for.

Open Plan

I imagined it differently, though I asked
for this: unlike the builder, I can't see what shapes
the future takes. Now these rooms paraphrase
my designs – perhaps something ungolden
in the ratio. I don't know geometry. The house
is nowhere, I can always be seen: glass
thaws the walls, the children are visible,
and do not forget how they need me. Standing
each afternoon over the butcher's offer
I view the leisure rooms in the splashback's
high gloss. How many years will I watch
reverse TV? Evenings I butterfly
a shoulder of lamb and drawers close
as they please. Sometimes I am almost at home.
When I saw men lift these benchtops
into place I thought of antiquity, marble statues
on streets in Greece and wondered if,
like gods, they might free me from my life.

Biking the Island

Sweated for hours on parched tar
where tour buses overtook. Slow
as shepherds we walked
our bikes beside her: she'd lied.
Spasms of light and distance bullied
her until she threw down
the bike. She wanted to revive
our girlhood: years since I looted
her little treasures for my bigger pile.
As always I had only cruelty to dispense,
would have left her there with lizards
under the sun's mandate
but you volunteered, took her
on your back. The buses rolled past us
in that vast blanched place.
Now and then brown rivets
of shrub in clay. I saw the tract
of sweat where her legs hooked
your hips. She gripped you
as if she was owed what is mine, what I
own. My love, I try to repair
what I break: sometimes
it takes years. As you know.

Homebody

Often we kicked it down at the cooldocks
where ships dragged in on coalish weather
and you'd get drunk, piss in the river.
Having nothing better to do I saw fit
to spend my life split:
embarrassment and ecstasy. It was easy,
then, being twenty. I didn't discern
my body's movement through time.
Now, having learned, I've turned back
to cities you shrugged off. Yes, you'd gloss this
as fear, my essential sin, and try to provoke
its twin, my rage. You'll never
move me again either way.

DAVID HAYDEN
MARRICKVILLE LIGHT

David Hayden was born in Ireland
and lives in England. His writing has
appeared in *Granta*, *A Public Space*,
Zoetrope All-Story, *The White Review*,
AGNI and *The Georgia Review*. His
first book, *Darker With the Lights On*,
was an *Irish Times* 'Book of the Year'.

AUSTRALIAN VOICES REMIND KATE OF DEAD PEOPLE. The people she loved as a child, who loved sun and ciggies. More than life itself, as it turned out. A large cup of syrupy black coffee was on the bench table. Her left hand was bunched in a fist to conceal a dozen or so almonds. She pinched out a couple with the fingers of her right hand and passed them to her mouth, crunched and chewed, and took a drink. Cassie sat next to her, hands in the pocket of her leather jacket, waiting for her tea to cool.

'Al came back from Adelaide months ago. Hasn't called anyone.'

'She in Marrickville?' asked Kate.

'Who knows? Wouldn't have thought so. Too pricy.'

'She back at uni?'

'Not that anyone's heard.'

'You could ask Jeannie.'

'Don't speak to Jeannie much these days.'

'Who could blame you?'

Kate gazed through the window into the neat courtyard. A stunted, bushy olive tree with silver-green leaves, two tall lime trees with fat twisted boughs, pale green, radiant in the winter sunlight. A woman in dirty chef whites and ragged blue-check trousers leaned against a leaf-shadowed wall, smoking a rollie. She looked up directly into Kate's face, smiled, took a long, slow drag, and held her gaze. Kate wanted to touch the frame of her reading glasses but stopped herself. A moment later she touched their right arm and passed her hand through her hair. The chef threw her cigarette end into an empty flowerbed and walked away and around the corner, hands in her pockets.

'How do you get a new life anyway?' said Cassie.

'Isn't that why you went to London?'

'Which worked out so well for everyone.'

'You going home?'

'Don't tell me you're not thinking the same.'

'I didn't say I wasn't...Actually, wasn't that just what I was saying. Kind of.'

'Just don't expect it to be home when you get back.'

'Wherever you go, there you are.'

'Thanks for that, mate.'

'You know what,' said Kate, 'I'm not even sure which home we're talking about.'

'Me too.'

'Better stay here then,' said Kate.

'Well, *I* want you around, anyhow, you ungrateful bastard,' said Cassie.

Kate's phone buzzed and clattered on the glass counter in the kitchen, Cassie's rumbled in her pocket. Cassie read hers first.

'It's Al.'

Kate reached her phone.

'Illawarra Road. Phở Thủy Tinh.'

Cassie rose.

'Let's take my car.'

The restaurant was little more than a family front room, with six tables and a dozen white plastic chairs, and a woman sat alone out of the late afternoon sun that cut through the blinds.

'I would like it if I were not unloveable,' she said. 'I always say too much.'

Cassie looked away, frustrated. But the room, sun-raked and simply beloved, seemed to agree that Al could be held for a while, but must, after no great passage of time, depart from the cheer and leave for the street, where the crowds were not waiting for her.

'But that's stupid,' said Kate. 'We love you.'

'I missed you,' said Cassie.

'Thank you, but I know that you enjoy my company for a while. And then an unnameable desperation begins to creep over you, and you'd do anything to be elsewhere, anywhere, than in a room with, across a table from, in a bed with me.'

Denial was not possible out of Kate's ingenuous face.

'You're very low, Al,' said Cassie.

'Where have you been?'

Three bowls of duck phở were placed on the table.

'I arrived with my luggage. I looked online in the taxi. There was too much choice and nothing I could afford. The real estate agent was alone in the office. She told me of a new property that had come available that afternoon. I was distracted by her red dress, her red hairband, the red necklace, the red bangle on her left arm, and when she stood, her green flats. She locked the office and walked me over, her moving quickly, me following slowly, haltingly, with my backpack and pull-along. I lost track of the time, but it was almost dark when we arrived outside an Italianate house, formerly a home for unwell mothers, which she said had recently been converted into apartments. They had been let all at once to a group of international students, who had departed, all at once, with no notice. We entered the lobby, which was very grand, dressed in grey veined Calacatta marble, illuminated with brass uplighters, and hastened up the blue carpeted staircase to the third floor. She spoke quickly in an undertone and apologised for the lack of an elevator. We passed

47

one broad brushed steel door after another down a long corridor until we reached the end. We stood outside. Her hand moved inside the large leather bag that was slung over her shoulder. And stopped.

'She handed me the keys and said, given my circumstances, which I had not described, I could move in tonight, without a deposit, the paperwork to be sorted out tomorrow. Or, perhaps, not tomorrow, because tomorrow was Sunday. Monday. She began to tell me that she had an event to go to, but broke off, turned around and walked at speed, just short of running, back down the corridor.

'I opened the door and an immensity of white light burst in, a phosphorescence that passed through every strand and particle of me. I thought there must be a row of klieg lights unaccountably arranged some distance ahead. I struggled to put on my sunglasses and, even then, I had to squint hard to look around. The apartment was furnished but had no blinds, no curtains. The light was coming from outside.'

Cassie began eating. There must have been the best part of half a duck in the bowl.

'I dropped my bags. The door was closed behind me. I walked to the window. My body seemed to vibrate in the light, but the room was cool. There was no sign of night outside, no sign of life in motion. The trees were silver, the asphalt ash-white, the bricks and steel, the concrete and the glass of the buildings were oyster white and palest grey. Colour had fallen out of the world.

'I felt tired beyond endurance and sat down in an armchair that faced out to the picture window and the street. I thought I would fall asleep, but I found that the tremor in my bones, my organs, through my skin, held me in place, awake. I did not

48

want to move, or think, or feel anything except this hovering frequency, this deep oscillation that harmonized with the radiance of the world.'

Al began to eat. Kate began to eat. Cassie had almost finished.

'This is so delicious,' she said.

The server returned with plastic tumblers of ice water.

'Thank you so much,' said Al, and she smiled as she looked into the woman's face.

'Are you...?' started Kate.

'My phone rang in my pocket,' said Al. 'Light collapsed all around into darkness that was thick, tarry, that soaked into my clothes and pushed into my eyes, my ears, my mouth, and, for what seemed like minutes, I couldn't breathe. My phone stopped ringing. It started again. I began to see the outlines of the room, the trees, the buildings outside, and I answered. It was Jeannie.'

Cassie looked across to the television, that sagged on the restaurant wall, where a contestant had one minute to make the audience laugh. The door opened and Jeannie walked in and across to their table.

Al drank from the tumbler, set it down on the placemat and spoke, loud and bright over the noise of the café.

'Do you want to come back to my apartment?'

ELLA SKILBECK-PORTER
FOUR POEMS

Ella Skilbeck-Porter is a writer and poet living on unceded Wurundjeri Country in Naarm/Melbourne. She is a PhD candidate in French Studies at the University of Melbourne and is currently working on her first collection of poetry, *These Are Different Waters*, which was shortlisted for the 2021 Helen Anne Bell Poetry Bequest. Her work has appeared in journals such as *Cordite*, *Rabbit*, *Runway*, *Going Down Swinging* and *Otoliths*.

Harbour

The harbours outside the window
are now inside

transplanted to the rosy sky
from a day in bed that becomes

every other day in bed
weather that is neutral and calm

passes in a feline way I keep
the same hours as the cats

or the cats keep the same hours
as me sheltering grief, pregnancy

a general malaise that is bone-deep
and flourishing like water in cells.

The frame relinquishes to gravity
and cares for what it loves

holding memories, a forming body
how many times can you write

I'm tired and am always in a different
city while walking the same street

it reaches the point where my inner map
is unreliable – unsure even of the hemisphere

I'm in. It is drizzling and I'm walking
along the canal to a job nannying

when I kick a pool of water
that sends forth a vertical jet stream

I am as amazed at the display
as the couple walking

towards me – the three of us sharing
the wordless moment.

Another common disorientation:
I walk into the supermarket to find

aisles in a new formation and me
with a basket in place of us with a trolley

we would sometimes lob the
speciality Cheeses of the World

into paper bags and pass them off as
button mushrooms to later feast

like kings, giddy with the self-created
feeling of majesty

See? A memory can be epiphany.
I feed the bed of roses banana skins

and clip the old buds back to the next
five-leaf leaflet. When a rose loses

its petals, a star calyx remains. Green
shadow that the flower blooms from.

When I walk through the house
I expect other rooms to appear

Do you understand that they do?

Herb Greedy Avenue, Marrickville

I trip up the slow avenue
I didn't realise I was in a different city
I didn't realise I can't sit down
That really is staggering
It blooms alongside of me
The wisteria and giant zucchini
which takes on the name of marrow
Carving it alone
In the marrow of it
This avenue isn't too long

Cat's Pantoum

Cat in curve, perched on the side table
She said, holding out her hand
House cat leans forward, leaps:
A dislocation finds its moment

She said, holding out her hand
Memories are and are not exact
A dislocation finds its moment
Can the experiment be summarised?

Memories are and are not exact
By experiment, a mean a desire to break
Can the experiment be summarised?
I cannot say it in a few words

By experiment, a mean a desire to break
And we have not proceeded, Sir,
I cannot say it in a few words
To want the same but different order

And we have not proceeded, Sir,
Still, walking back is elusive
To want the same but different order
Circularising modes of attention

Still, walking back is elusive
Cat in curve, perched on the side table
Circularising modes of attention
The cat curves into the fold

Two Days After Samhain

What a luxury
to have coffee and dates
in bed

to not worry about
rising late on a
Tuesday

to stroke the hair
on my chin and consider
painting

a portrait of the scene
though I don't have a
monobrow

I draw in the cats
the roses the coffee
I am

drinking the five dates
that I'm eating, the child
swimming

the field of lavender
parting the house from
the street

now purple purple
purple when recently
just grey

I thought them ruined
from my neglect but here
they are

wild, not needing
intervention, take the lesson
watching

As the rosemary goes
to seed, May turns mauve
flowers

A year in a house
a protective spell
casting

LUKE BEESLEY
TWO STORIES

Luke Beesley is a poet, artist and singer-songwriter. His most recent poetry collection, *Aqua Spinach*, was shortlisted for the ALS Gold Medal. His poetry has been published widely in Australia and internationally and has been translated into several languages. He lives and works on Wurundjeri Woi Wurrung land (Melbourne).

Time Piece

I was rushing out of the house in the morning. The night before, I'd calculated the time it would take to drive out around peak hour next morning. It was. And the traffic canted into intersections via assumed breeze, invisible momentum that took me back to a very small childhood fear of the day's adult inevitability. Or perhaps it was more about onrush: each adult in their not-so-much uncaring but distracted trajectories, en masse, racing forward, and that dawning, really, on a young person.

In primary school I would fear assemblies. Kids emerging from classrooms to form endless concrete-grey and blue lines that happened to be, these years later, the same colour of the cars that slid forwards – traffic right-to-left ungainly against the momentum of these sentences. I can sense, as I leave the house –

see, the inevitability of writing, its pressure. The sharpened nib decisive, flaking in the morning's axis (that chance).

I am to spend the day at a full stop. The cars stop, and we are given the opportunity to wash them. I find I have a sponge in my hand when I jot these thoughts down. It is heavy already with soupy water: a kidney-shaped sponge much like the colour of the lines at the top of this page – pink-ruled lines above thin-blue veins below. Or, I should say, a thin vein-blue where I enter and join the rush of traffic.

I'd quickly decided, next day – this one – that I would see if my friend Daniel Read was free to play tennis. I was able to organise this easily. The idea congealed in a carpark. SUVs reversing nicely, the sun glinting off their metallic sides as they swivelled. A mini had snuck in like the dog or kid or goof in romantic comedy, to lighten things, and we laughed.

But who are 'we'? I guess there – from childhood, and even in the womb, I don't know – begins an oval. Theatre in the round. And we, us, are the potential. Inertia with momentum.

The previous evening I was reading a poem where the repeated word 'shadow' (x3) was used to mimic the sound of the heart. Clever. There is not much we can hide underneath a coin. Eventually there is a system beneath the 'manhole' on the footpath, but it takes some time for this to emerge. Lovely mystery. That labyrinth, as it happens, must be part of the frightening 'we' that we carry around on our peripheries, that laughs or withholds change. Withholds change! When the traffic-light window washer decides to give you a windscreen wash, after all, to coax you, despite you miming no. *That* feeling.

What I failed to mention was that Read – when I asked if he was free on this Friday – asked if, before tennis and a coffee, or coffee and tennis (it turned out to occur after our black stovetop coffee and before tennis), I would help him move a boulder.

Read had not long before moved to the small town of Full Stop, and his house on the outskirts – a truck-transported old schoolhouse – tilted down the valley. He had been working on the landscape, collecting native trees and choreographing at the house's margin. He had shaped what we might call *the pencil of his attitude* using books on theory – behaviour change – learning to sit with an old poet friend for an hour to explain the clunky nature, the dimples, of the rocks themselves.

They were rocks within rocks – ha! Pebbles seemingly attached to the outside of his memory, or was it therapy? Barnacles. Bare-knuckled, we were to twist the rock, together, using the limits of our empathy, for it had been a long time since we'd seen each other.

Read, later that day, leveraged the rock with a crowbar. My hands twisted swiftly, opening a bottle of fizzy water, ninety-degree angle, into the town, searching for shade given we were to play tennis later in the day and I was concerned for my racquet's string tension etc., and I grazed my palm. Two round red wounds the size of a watch battery. They bled, but not too much – for most of the morning they were wet circles.

Immediately, unseeing, Read suggested another angle, permutation; he was so profoundly concentrating on our conversation, I think, that he hadn't noted that I'd grazed my hand in small, watch-battery-sized ways, and I'd only glanced at my hand, at that point, like quickly checking the time itself, so I'd not fully registered the wound, and there was an old school day swimming to my memory, or back further – insecurity – or was it a gesture to show that I too had lived in the country, knew of pain, that my muscles hadn't metastasised. An instinct to push on, ignore the pain. We *did* eventually arrange that rock into a plan that Read was comfortable with. He had just told me a sequence of irritating events: his car had slipped out of registration – lapsed is the word I'm looking for. Also, his neighbours were moving out and their dog was resisting acupuncture. Read's brother, too, had chronic pain and his health had spiralled.

I was sitting on Read's couch with said stovetop coffee, listening, when he paused for quite some time. He pointed to a sapling he had planted the week before but that had been overwhelmed by treatment, fading to a pale version of itself. When I write treatment, I mean to intuit the word, our conversation, and the conversations had by people all over the small town we sat on the edge of: an imperceptible form of consciousness of the populace itself.

But who needs *it?* We ask, and yet it is addictive. The breeze picking up, pushing through a flyscreen and tickling the very fine hairs on my ear. Something I didn't even notice!

But who are *we?* When you drive in towards a valley town, morning, and the light is still settling itself, purple. When the sun is stretching to the chrome, acting on an origin-yellow, or orange, is when you begin to know a collective. But then again, often, that frisson, cinematic, is not quite the location of the town anyway. Just a collection of trees by a river – a fleeting battery-powered elegance, but you have moved on by then and shaped your life around it.

Read cried. Or I wondered if he shed a tear. It was a twist in emotional grammar – subtle anguish, real elegance, the sun turning – and I paraphrased hard, hearing him out. He knew none of this would add up, but I showed him the face of my watch anyway. I offered him the chance to push a few buttons, make a calculation, and we finished our coffee and decided to move the rock before heading to tennis.

Cartoon Lake

I was sitting on a park bench in winter waiting for my spine to register the chill. The sun was on the side of my face, and I could hear a soccer match. I tried to follow each player without looking at the oval; the players scattered and flickered, and I wanted to be the literature, the story – was sick of merely gusting at the side of it. I figured the first step would be to get cold, to be still, and yet activate a thought. To run my fingers.

The players set off and stretched in a ballet-twist. Or I tried to hold myself elegantly like tai chi, standing, supporting myself with one hand and shuffling close to the corner post, well into the outline of the oval. I kept my eyes closed, curious about the overflow of material movement nibbling at the out-edge of what was a pool. Animals – birds and striped horses, cats with sandy beards, a quick rusty leaf upturned and gliding beside a frantic lip.

Way up in the arctic regions there was a group of 'men and women' prepared to map what was, at the time, an A4 page. They took fine scissors and with elaborate sunglasses laughed at their own reflections: women and men who sliced through the ice and snow and arrived with pens and rulers and soothed the barren contours, always imagining the land mass below the ice. They moved forward and held up stainless-steel cups and rented cars as soon as they got back to the airport.

They'd returned completely stumped by the routine of a manual car. One hand went out to steer, the other westwards to mark the changing of the days, as if they could shuffle between those days (as they seemed to do, out on the ice).

One day followed another until they were home wiping

their feet on a cat, or cars whining by like the sound of a cat. Cats daring to skip across the streets between cars, and shadows tempting drivers to follow them in the corner of the drivers' eyes. They, these shadows, were tranquilisers – long sharp darts kept in padded stainless-steel pods (in the glovebox). The dart made a decompressed gulp through the air as the animals lifted their donkey heads, suddenly hit, and folded. Cats squeezed past the tiny round legs of the men and women wiping their feet courteously on the cats escaping, polishing their shoes up beautifully. Orange cats squirting past, like ink, a splash cartoonists make!

All this, an act of mapping the land.

I itched my hand. I itched my head with the end of my pencil and ran the pencil along the page itching and bothering away, ten and twenty times or more looking up to commit a line against my own reflection. It took off below a crease that had emerged a decade earlier below the very ballpoint of my eye – that little step towards where tadpoles leapt, stretching across the open upper face.

Fold marks. As if you could turn your eye in, brittle on a piece of musk. And relief – massage. Steaming hot day and the masseuse runs an ice cube along the upper outline of your eyebrow following it away from your eye. Mist caught in the branches. Below lower branches of the trees, young parents run up and down the touchline with exaggerated arms, throwing them in opposites to the slow stretch that is the line out over exercise, or, I should say, I'm writing about soccer.

It's half time.

Oranges severed in examples of the subject. Mouth-sized sections stinging at the corner of the mouth, the writing went. Squinting across the page in flung pebbles to attract the attention of, or to disturb, a body of water represented by a large sky-blue stain off the side of a town marked by a single freckle.

I have a mole on the inside of my hand, see, which sits at the centre of the story.

I feel guilty about my mood, which is scattered and listless. In truth, the waterhole is a gravy brown. Ribs stretch striped thick loose skin of the zebras, and I'm walking across the road. I'm on a traffic island in the middle of Punt Road with a takeaway coffee. I'm on the island for three gulps, and the traffic passes me the way theatregoers find their seats, squeezing past tucked legs, brushing and excusing themselves as we hold our calves close to the plush red seats before stretching them out again and turning our phones off, allowing the stage lights to brush over us – an aeroplane passing overhead, its pale underbelly. We even dribble! Our thoughts disperse and our mind is left dripping – not a ripple. Breeze. A few birds scribble back and across, but its otherwise a show of quietude. I'm on my stomach, peering through the hole in my Frisbee. I see a building going up across the street and kids washing cars with a toothbrush. The silly tickling arm of an excavator, bright flecks of orange and yellow on the chests of the workers, would spin and ricochet off the long glass doors of our apartment block beyond us. I try to catch my reflection in those doors. I am on my stomach, and finally the subject.

Now and then I look up to the soccer or swivel sideways to scratch my stomach or realise I'm adhered to the illusion-point that text makes at the top right corner of the page.

I'm looking up now and then, from a book, to imagine a printed page.

I have my eye on soccer and it pulls in its socket. I'm drawn towards it like a tug – rubbery noisette with the wide wristy-thick metal cable in its mouth, bobbing and whipping and copying, oscillating, pages riddled and folded and placed in envelopes and posted back to my open palm, reaching at the limit of a stretch – pinned up the side, across the back, in the park.

AMY LEACH
AMEN TO NONSENSE

Amy Leach lives in Montana and is the author of *Things That Are* and *The Everybody Ensemble*. Her work has appeared in *The Best American Essays*, *The Best American Science and Nature Writing* and numerous other publications, including *Granta* and *A Public Space*. She has been recognised with a Whiting Award and a Rona Jaffe Foundation Writers' Award.

DIRT BEING SO GENERAL, it's strange that it gets turned into singular things, like the pumpkin on my table, the fly on the pumpkin rubbing her front legs together, me. I was born with an antipathy to generalisation and everything I experienced subsequent to parturition exacerbated that antipathy. Still, there are a few generalisations I can go along with, like 'Everything that exists is good,' as St Augustine wrote, and 'Everything that lives is holy,' like William Blake said. I would add, 'Everything that lives is dirty.' There goes a good holy dirty dermatology resident, here comes a good dirty holy mole.

The other day I saw a whole holy family – parents, a toddler, a baby, grandparents, and a probable auntie – out walking their holy hedgehog. It was on a leash and the family was trying to walk down the sidewalk, but the hedgehog kept scuttling into the bushes, perhaps hoping to snarf down an insect. The forward trajectory of the family plus the sideways trajectory of the hedgehog made for slow going. (In the hedgehog's mind *she* was the one going forward and the *people* were going sideways.)

Another acceptable generalisation is 'Person is dogged by death.' Just yesterday a truck reading 'Gutter Solutions' nearly ran me over. En route to solving someone's gutter problems, that truck nearly caused a different, insoluble problem. Person is perishable like grass. *The life of mortals is like grass, they flourish like a flower of the field.* Person is pretty and perishable like flower.

My daughter calls herself Pastor Petunia and I think it suits her because, while many pastors put me in a refutational mood, this tiny pastor is irrefutable like a petunia. Actually all flowers are irrefutable like petunias – tulips, dandelions, gazanias, mandevillas, snapdragons, broccolis. Try refuting any of them:

stand a buttercup on one podium and stand yourself at another podium and try to defeat her with your logic. Argue, argue, contend and contest, but the buttercup will not be refuted, although by the time you are finished she may be droopy.

Sometimes I feel like a general flower – momentary – and sometimes I feel like a particular flower, like the marvel-of-Peru, also known as the four o'clock flower, who snoozes all day until late in the afternoon when she finally gets around to opening up her petals. Sometimes I feel like a watermelon flower: preliminary. Nobody laments the fading of the watermelon flower.

Some days my life feels extremely preliminary. I had the sense this morning, after I left the children at school and walked the puppy in the October sunshine, that this moment was in the distant past, that the aspen leaves so radiant yellow had already fallen to the ground, turned dull brown, disintegrated. We had already carved the pumpkin into a jack-o'-lantern, which had already started to look old – scarred and wrinkled and slumpy-faced – had already rotted and moulded and gotten tossed out behind the fence and turned back into dirt. The cows in the field behind my house had long ago been trucked off to a slaughterhouse. Those cow songs always sounded sad to me.

The high school juniors out on the trail with their notebooks, taking nature notes for English class, had graduated, gone to college, gotten married, had children, begun to look like old jack-o'-lanterns, had passed on. A long time ago the puppy had stopped chewing up our books and boots and dollies, had stopped barking at shadows, had grown accustomed to shadows, had slowed down, hips gone rickety, had died. My parents were gone and I was gone, and my children had had children who'd had children who'd had children, and my name was on a long list of somebody's great-great-great-great-great-great-great-great-great-great-great-grandparents.

I thought I was walking the dog on a chilly October morning, but it was all over. The crick in my neck had gone away, I had made bread later in the afternoon, or not, had gotten around to reading Herodotus, or not, had found my lost knitting needle so I could finish the blue scarf I'd started knitting last fall, or not, had perished from crashing or fire or cancer or time. Time cleaned my clock, if nothing else did.

Presidents had succeeded presidents, screeds had succeeded screeds, people trying their damnedest had given way to other people trying their damnedest. Some things are up for grabs, like jobs and dollars and votes, and are worth trying one's damnedest for, and some things are not, like time and the moon and the stars. The Bible was always saying to 'lift up your eyes', maybe because when we lifted our eyes we remembered that not everything was up for grabs. (When they named ages they usually named them after grabbable things, like iron, stone, bronze, information, etc., not ungrabbable things like the moon and the stars.)

Pythagoras had been a cucumber in a former life, so he had that extra cucumber perspective on things. He had also been a sardine. Pythagoras the cucumber, Pythagoras the sardine, Pythagoras the person – Pythagoras knew there are some things you just have to roll with. If you are a cucumber, for example, you have to roll with your greenness, bumpiness, bulbousness, coolness – and, if you are of the Intimidator variety of cucumber, your intimidatingness.

My former lives are a little blurry to me but I'm trying to roll with this one – my toothiness, nosiness, spindliness, humanity, my age, and I like to think of my age as the Moon Age, for it's as moony as any other age, maybe moonier, since it's a moon-going age. I am guessing I never go there *myself*, though, except for musically. I *have* been to the moon in song.

I've ridden ponies in the mountains of Lesotho and played the violin in Slovakia and visited the haunts of the little blue fairy penguin in New Zealand. I've been to Brazil, where I was put in prison and given pizza. But the farthest I've ever travelled was when listening to Bach's pieces for unaccompanied violin. An *accompanied* violinist has somebody providing the chords, context, atmosphere, rhythm, and background for her melody. Everything is spelled out, and all a listener has to do is sit in his chair and listen. But the unaccompanied violinist, who can play only one or two notes at a time, has to *imply* all the notes she's not playing, and the listener has to *imagine* those unplayed notes. Made up so largely of implication, Bach's Chaconne forces us to be fathomers.

Of course not everybody appreciates having to be a fathomer. Some people prefer to have everything spelled out. John Cook wrote: 'The Chaconne is sublimely satisfying in its original form, yet many will agree that a single violin is only able to hint at the vast implications of much of this music...' Because of that word 'yet', it sounds to me like Mr Cook is *not* sublimely satisfied with the original form, that actually he'd prefer a Chaconne transcribed for the organ, a transcription that dispensed with hints and vast implications and made everything explicit. Personally I prefer the original version, the moon and star of it.

Or maybe I do go to the Moon and not just musically. Maybe when I am eighty I win a go-to-the-Moon lottery and I like it so much I say *I'm never going back*. But I doubt it because there's no music there, or rather, the music on the Moon is *all implication*, since they don't have any medium to convey sound. Another thing is that the Moon isn't very funny. The Moon and the Red Planet and the Yellow-Brown Planet and the Teal Planet are all grand-venerable-portentous but if you want a good laugh you have to go to the Blue Planet, which I think of as the Froggy Planet or the Piggy Planet or the Planty Planet. It could also be called the Nonsense Planet, since it's the only planet with nonsense rats. Nonsense rats live on Trinket Island in the Indian Ocean.

Holst's suite *The Planets* has movements for Mercury, Venus, Mars, Jupiter, Saturn, Uranus, and Neptune, but no movement for the Earth, probably because the Earth is piggy and turtly and ridiculous. For an idea of what it would sound like if Holst had included a movement for Earth, try listening to *The Planets*, but in between 'Mars' and 'Venus', insert *The Carnival of the Animals* by Saint-Saëns, featuring cuckoos, kangaroos, tortoises dancing the cancan, and 'People with Long Ears'. People with long ears are donkeys. (People are donkeys with short ears.)

Holst's suite was performed in public but Saint-Saëns only allowed his suite to be performed privately while he was alive because he thought it was frivolous. It is funny for dirt to write music and then think it frivolous. It is also funny for dirt to write serious music. It is funny for dirt to be musical, moody, wordy, wiggly, brainy, spleeny, hearty. It is funny for dirt to be a sourpuss or have a bubbly personality or a saggy personality or a starchy personality or a personality at all. It is funny for dirt to futz around or go bananas or go by Frank. It's funny for dirt to get irritated by dirt on the kitchen floor; funny for dirt to invent banshees, funny for dirt to banish the banshees. It is funny for dirt to be a duck or a poppy or a Venezuelan poodle moth or to address its own planet, as did Walt Whitman: 'Say, old top-knot, what do you want?'

Along with the hens and kangaroos and wild asses, piano players get their own movement in *The Carnival of the Animals*, and the piano animals fit right in with the rest of the animals. I live with two piano animals, one of whom plays 'Jolly Old St. Nicholas' over and over every afternoon when she comes home from school. Before she started playing it constantly I hadn't realised that the melody is really a heartbreaker. The other pianist plays Reveille at six o'clock in the morning, to try and wake up the lazy bums in his house. He does not sing these lyrics but powerfully implies them:

I can't get 'em up
I can't get 'em up
I can't get 'em up this morning;
I can't get 'em up
I can't get 'em up
I can't get 'em up at all!

In the Chaconne, the notes you can hear imply the notes you can't hear; I'd say the ratio of present notes to absent notes is about one to four. It is a propulsive ratio: I once heard an ancient wispy-haired man playing the Chaconne and was propelled out beyond Cassiopeia. (They called the sixties the Space Age but I say Bach's age was the Space Age too.) Songs with mostly present notes are not as propulsive; they will not propel you into space, though they might propel you over the backyard fence, or almost over the fence.

Too many absent notes can be a problem, too, like in the songs they sing on the Moon. But even one note – especially if Count Basie is playing it – can imply scores of absent notes. A little can imply a lot, like how one itty-bitty fossil tooth found along the Río Alto Madre de Dios implies all those hamster-sized monkeys bouncing around Peru eighteen million years ago. If micromonkey tooth, then micromonkeys.

If scarf, then knitter. If egg, then egret. If you, then your parents. If you didn't know your parents you could still infer them from your existence and if you didn't know about the stars you could similarly infer them from yourself. You can examine your composition – your carbon and magnesium and gold and silicon – and extrapolate the stars, because to forge those heavy elements there obviously had to be several generations of stars going kerblooey. I mean I assume you are a person but if you are a flamingo you could equally extrapolate the stars (and your parents).

In a former life I may have been a cucumber, my elements contributing to one of those Indian cucumbers three thousand years ago. I wonder if I was an intimidating cucumber. I've probably been grasses, probably goats, possibly doodlebugs, but I know for sure I was an asteroid. I like to remember that life as an asteroid because it helps me remember this life – the one that feels like having feet so cold I can't sleep, like getting dragged face first through the sand by a labrador retriever, like using an oven mitt with a hole in it so my fingers get burned, like letting the toddlers in the backseat pull cattails apart, filling the car with fluff, like getting a little tipsy on pinot grigio while one piano animal plays a throbbing rhythm on the piano – ONE-and-two-AND-three-and-FOUR-and-ONE-and-two-AND-three-and-FOUR-and – and the other piano animal spins me around in an old blue chair.

Now that he's perennially playing that rhythm it's my favourite rhythm, right behind triple time, and although I don't like summaries, if I had to summarise my life I would call it The Acquisition of Appreciation. I used to be narrow-minded and did not appreciate 'Jolly Old St. Nicholas'; I used to be conventional and thought that only ladies with supple legs should dance the cancan, but now I enjoy it when tortoises dance it too.

I used to think that famous people were more important than other people, but now that I have gotten to know so many people who aren't famous, I have changed my mind. I know somebody who isn't famous who gave me her old mixer. I know another person who isn't famous who gave us four little bicycles her children had outgrown. No famous person has ever given me a bicycle or a mixer.

I didn't used to love Iowa or Ornette Coleman or the sound of French. I didn't used to appreciate goat-sounding singers, till one summer evening in the Adirondacks I heard a woman who sang like a goat singing 'Hard Times Come Again No More' and I swear no woman-voiced woman has ever made me cry like that. I didn't used to think that people who look like toads are beautiful but that's definitely where I have ended up – *person is pretty like toad*. I assume that with time I will accumulate more and more appreciations until by the time I die I will love even blue cheese and Charles Dickens and summaries and politics and the winds in Livingston, Montana.

The world is appreciating for me – getting dearer with time. Something else that's appreciating with time is time, and another thing is nonsense, especially as nonsense is so vulnerable these days. Nonsense rats became endangered after the 2004 tsunami, and if nonsense rats go extinct then the world will be a little less nonsensical, a little more like Neptune, more of a candidate for *The Planets*. I define nonsense as everything that is unimplied by the stars. Though we imply the stars, the stars do not imply us – not if we're human, or flamingo, or cucumber – nor any of the other Earthly etceteras. If you'd been raised among the stars and nobody'd ever told you about the Earth, what about the stars would lead you to conclude that all their exploding had resulted in chipmunks? Chipmunks are curveballs. Chipmunks are surprise chipmunks.

Humans are surprise humans and if the stars do not imply humans then they really do not imply Schopenhauer, or Fats Domino, or Geronimo, or Rickey Smith, or that Rickey Smith would sing 'I Believe I Can Fly' with such intensity we all believed he could fly too, or that instead of flying he'd be killed by a drunk driver headed the wrong way on an Oklahoma highway early one morning in 2016. The stars *do* plausibly imply the rings of Saturn: blasted into space by a supernova, dust predictably coalesces into asteroids and asteroids predictably coalesce into planets and planets not unpredictably collect disks of dust. Saturn's rings, being predictably circly, dusty, and disky are not nonsense like Earth's rings, made of space junk.

Saturn is also predictably moony, much moonier than Earth. Saturn has fifty-three confirmed moons and twenty-nine provisional moons 'awaiting confirmation'. (Saturn is keeping some moons under his hat. Like other characters compensating

81

for their lack of funniness, Saturn tries to maintain a certain 'mystique'.) Anyway, to be moony and provisionally moony all you have to be is massy, but to be loony and limpety and shrimpy and shrewy and eely and yakky and oaky and doodlebuggy and snapdragonny and buttercuppy and honeysuckly and hippopotamussy, being massy is not enough.

I might also define nonsense as anything beautiful, like toads and rats and hogs, those heartstoppers. Some people, like Walt Whitman, are in hog heaven here, among all the beauty; Whitman and the Earth got along like a house on fire. But for other people, beauty is not their cup of tea, and they say to anything beautiful, *You can't 'come hither' me!* They are hog-proof, sheep-proof, mushroom-proof – Earth-proof, in fact, like those buttercup debunkers – *buttercups are so bogus* – who, when the debunking doesn't work, may put on their flight gear and get in their bombers and fly around bombing the buttercups. If you can't debunk something you can still bomb it.

The problem with blitzing flowers is that flowers are always reappearing, like remember how after the Blitz all that ragwort and fireweed popped up in London? I've walked through a burned forest where all the trees were charred and black and sensibly you'd expect on the ground an ashy nothingness but it was full of nonsensically pink fireweed, and nonsensically sweet raspberries. After tasting one raspberry, the baby pressed her fellow hikers into feeding her raspberries for the rest of the hike. The baby is not raspberryproof. One raspberry turns the baby into a raspberry despot and everyone around her into conscripts.

Keats wrote that 'Twang dillo dee' – which means 'amen to nonsense' – should be written across the backs of politicians and 'at the end of most modern Poems' and on all American books, and that 'Twang dillo dee' is *actually inscribed* across our planet: 'Some philosophers in the Moon who spy at our Globe as we do at theirs say that Twang dillo dee is written in large Letters on our Globe of Earth.' When I was musically visiting the Moon I looked back at Earth and I saw it! I saw how the vertical line of the 'T' traces the Rocky Mountains, how the 'g' of the 'wang' lies mostly over the ocean but catches, slightly, the coast of Mauritania, how the 'd' of the 'dee' curves around Sulawesi. Like John Keats, I say amen to nonsense, but my amen is sincere, and to reformulate one of his formulations, I say, '"Beauty is Nonsense, Nonsense Beauty." – that is all / Ye know on earth, and all ye need to know.'

Except, this definition of nonsense would *include* the planets and stars, however humourless, for they are very beautiful – sparkly scarlet, glowy yellow, etc. If you'd been raised in a box and nobody had ever told you about the stars; if you'd been kept in the dark all your life but had doped out the stars' existence from studying your composition, wouldn't you still be shocked, upon being let out and lifting up your eyes? Extrapolated stars can't hold a candle to real stars. And if you lifted up your eyes would you ever even lower them again? Wouldn't you get all strung out on the stars? Maybe if we could only see the universe from far enough away – if we could listen to some song so propulsively composed as to pitch us out beyond the huddle of our universe – we'd spy 'Amen to Nonsense' written across the whole nonsensically pretty shebang.

Glossary

The Marvel of Peru. Hey, Marvel of Peru, wake up, it's four o'clock, you're the flower of the hour!

One of many great-great-great-great-great-grandparents. Perhaps my great-great-great-great-great-great-granddaughter shares with me my sloppiness and sleepiness, or maybe, with all those other ancestors contributing to her constitution, the attributes she received from me are tempered, moderated, rendered merely charming. Along with a little sleepiness and sloppiness and forgetfulness and gullibility she also possesses common sense and studiousness and resolve. I think she is perfect and am proud to have gone into her making.

Children who'd had children who'd had children. I am a first-generation violinist, a third-generation pianist, and a ten-thousandth-generation child.

Slumpy-faced. Jack-o'-lanterns really let themselves go.

Funny for dirt to be hearty and brainy. It is also funny for dirt to have no heart and no brain, like the starfish.

Funny for dirt to be hearty and brainy. It is funniest of all for dirt to be soully.

Propelled out beyond Cassiopeia. One thing I noticed while I was out there was that the stars were obeying Albert Einstein rather than Isaac Newton. If you want the stars to obey you, being a physicist is not enough – you also have to be a violinist.

Geronimo. What do you mean, 'Geronimo Who?' There's only one Geronimo. Have you ever heard anybody talking about the Geronimos?

Tulips and dandelions. Never has there been a wave of dandelionomania like that one wave of tulipomania in seventeenth-century Holland. Never has anyone given forty acres in exchange for one dandelion. However, as the price of dandelions has never risen, so their price has never crashed. The worth of dandelions is not bestowed upon them – nor is it removed – by the market. (Actually this is true of tulips too.)

Dandelionomania. I know two children who are dandelionomaniacs.

Chipmunks are curveballs. Chipmunks are unique among curveballs in that they pitch *themselves.* They are stripey little curveballs pitching themselves around the forest gathering hazelnuts in their cheeks.

Surprise chipmunks. Just ask the people who recently arrived on the planet how surprising chipmunks are.

Acceptable generalisations. Another one is 'Rabbi is bigger than rabbit.' The littlest rabbi is bigger than the biggest rabbit. Actually never mind, I forgot about Ralph. Ralph the Rabbit weighs forty-two pounds and is way bigger than a baby rabbi.

When I am eighty. Isn't a number a funny adjective to apply to a person, as in Anna Maria is nine, Andre is thirty-seven?

Lift up your eyes. 'Lift up your eyes' is different from 'Roll your eyes', although sometimes when I am rolling my eyes I happen to catch a glimpse of the stars and then I stop rolling my eyes and keep them lifted up.

If you are a flamingo. If you are a flamingo, you are very expensive, because so many stars had to be spent in the making of you!

If us, then stars. We *imply* the stars, and we also *employed* them. Weren't we clever to employ the stars in manufacturing our elements?

The stars do not imply us if we're flamingos. Extrapolating flamingos from the stars is like extrapolating Emily Dickinson's poems from the alphabet.

Accumulation of appreciation. Another thing accumulating for me is good choices. When I was young my choices were between good things and bad things. It is bad to smoke cigarettes and good to not smoke cigarettes: choose. It is bad to eat Cheetos and good to eat carrots: choose. Now almost all my choices are between good things and good things and good things and good things: it is good to do laundry and good to answer emails and good to read Dostoevsky and good to practice the violin: how to choose? Not smoking cigarettes is simple and easy, like being in a room with one squirrel and not sitting on it. But now I have to choose between all these good things where doing one of them means not doing another of them, like if I fold the laundry I'm not reading Dostoevsky and if I read Dostoevsky I'm not making soup and if I make soup then I'm not walking the dog, and I feel like I'm in a room with so many squirrels and not sitting on one squirrel means sitting on another squirrel and so all I ever do is sit on squirrels and apologise to squirrels.

Made of so much implication. There are books as well as songs whose implications fling you into space: Basho, Emily Dickinson, and the Book of Job come to mind. Also there are books whose gravity pulls you into orbit around them. *Leaves of Grass* is such a book, like a red hypergiant star – open it up and you will be permanently captured. Other books are like asteroids and can be safely cracked without fear of circling them for the rest of your life. You have to really try and orbit an asteroid.

Walt Whitman. Dead poets are sometimes dismissed because they are dead but I feel more dismissive of dead poems than dead poets.

Some books pull you into orbit. How much orbital power Flaubert possesses I do not know because I have never opened his books. Eleven years ago I bought *Bouvard and Pecuchet* but have yet to open it up, and nobody has ever made me read *Madame Bovary.*

Planty planet. Earth is the plantiest planet but not the planetiest planet. The word 'planet' comes from an old Greek word for 'wanderer', but the Earth, locked into its track around the sun, is not all that wandery. The really wandery planets are those rogue planets roaming the Milky Way, unattached to any star.

Buttercup debunkers. I feel that my calling is to counterbalance the buttercup debunkers. I do this by buttering up the buttercups.

New Titles from Giramondo

Fiction

George Alexander *Mortal Divide: The Autobiography of Yiorgos Alexandroglou*
Luke Carman *An Ordinary Ecstasy*
Norman Erikson Pasaribu *Happy Stories, Mostly* (trans. Tiffany Tsao)
Jessica Au *Cold Enough for Snow*
Max Easton *The Magpie Wing*
Zarah Butcher-McGunnigle *Nostalgia Has Ruined My Life*
Pip Adam *Nothing to See*

Non-fiction

Bastian Fox Phelan *How to Be Between*
Antigone Kefala *Late Journals*
Evelyn Juers *The Dancer: A Biography for Philippa Cullen*
Gerald Murnane *Last Letter to a Reader*
Anwen Crawford *No Document*
Vanessa Berry *Gentle and Fierce*

Poetry

Lisa Gorton *Mirabilia*
Zheng Xiaoqiong *In the Roar of the Machine* (trans. Eleanor Goodman)
Lionel Fogarty *Harvest Lingo*
Tracy Ryan *Rose Interior*
Claire Potter *Acanthus*
Adam Aitken *Revenants*
J.S. Harry *New and Selected Poems*
Andy Jackson *Human Looking*
Eunice Andrada *Take Care*
Jane Gibian *Beneath the Tree Line*

For more information visit giramondopublishing.com.

Subscribe Now

And receive each issue of HEAT

Australia's international literary magazine

Since its inception in 1996, HEAT has been renowned for a dedication to quality and a commitment to publishing innovative and imaginative poetry, fiction, essays and hybrid forms. Now, in the third series, we are excited to bring together a selection of the most interesting and adventurous Australian and overseas writers. HEAT Series 3 is posted to subscribers every two months, forming a unique, cohesive whole. Your subscription supports independent literary publishing, and enables us to cultivate and champion new and challenging writing.

Visit giramondopublishing.com/heat/ to subscribe.

Submission Guidelines

HEAT welcomes submissions of fiction, essays, poetry and translated works throughout the year. We encourage writing which gives full rein to the author's voice, without the restriction of a word limit. In the case of poetry, we seek longer poems, or a selection or sequence of poems. For further information, please visit our website.

Acknowledgements

We respectfully acknowledge the Gadigal, Burramattagal and Cammeraygal peoples, the traditional owners of the lands where Giramondo's offices are located. We extend our respects to their ancestors and to all First Nations peoples and Elders.

HEAT Series 3 Number 4 has been prepared in collaboration with Ligare Book Printers, Avon Graphics, Ball & Doggett paper suppliers and Candida Stationery; we thank them for their support.

The Giramondo Publishing Company is grateful for the support of Western Sydney University in the implementation of its book publishing program.

Giramondo Publishing is assisted by the Australian Government through the Australia Council for the Arts.

HEAT Series 3
Editor Alexandra Christie
Designer Jenny Grigg
Typesetter Andrew Davies
Copy Editor Aleesha Paz
Marketing and Publicity Manager Kate Prendergast
Editorial Intern Lucia Nguyen
Publishers Ivor Indyk and Evelyn Juers
Associate Publisher Nick Tapper

Editorial Advisory Board
Chris Andrews, Mieke Chew, J.M. Coetzee, Lucy Dougan, Lisa Gorton,
Bella Li, Tamara Sampey-Jawad, Suneeta Peres da Costa,
Alexis Wright and Ashleigh Young.

Contact
For editorial enquiries, please email
heat.editor@giramondopublishing.com.
Follow us on Instagram @HEAT.lit and
Twitter @HEAT_journal.

Accessibility
We understand that some formats will not be accessible to all readers.
If you are a reader with specific access requirements, please contact
orders@giramondopublishing.com.

For more information, visit giramondopublishing.com/heat.

Published August 2022
from the Writing and Society Research Centre
at Western Sydney University
by the Giramondo Publishing Company
PO Box 752
Artarmon NSW 1570 Australia
www.giramondopublishing.com

This collection © Giramondo Publishing 2022
Typeset in Tiempos and Founders Grotesk Condensed
designed by Kris Sowersby at Klim Type Foundry

Printed and bound by Ligare Book Printers
Distributed in Australia by NewSouth Books

A catalogue record for this book is available from
the National Library of Australia.

HEAT Series 3 Number 4
ISBN: 978-1-922725-03-5
ISSN: 1326-1460

ISBN 978-1-922725-03-5

9 781922 725035 >